NOTES TO MY FUTURE HUSBAND

A BITCH'S GUIDE TO OUR HAPPILY EVER AFTER

The Coquette

Published by Sourcebooks, Inc.
P.O. Box 4410, Naperville, Illinois 60567-4410
(630) 961-3900
Fax: (630) 961-2168
www.sourcebooks.com

CIP data is on file with the publisher.

Printed and bound in the United States of America.
VP 10 9 8 7 6 5 4 3 2

To the men who have asked to marry me.

CONTENTS

I am a picky bitch. No doubt you are, too. We belong to a lucky generation of American women who don't have to spend their early twenties in a mad dash to get hitched to the nearest breadwinner. It took three waves of feminism, a few landmark pieces of legislation, and a massive cultural shift toward gender equality, but tying the knot is no longer a prerequisite to leading a stable and happy life. Husbands are optional these days.

That's not to say we don't want one. We might. It's just nice not having to need one.

We get to seek independence and self-knowledge before seeking a life partner. We get to play the field like all the boys do. We get to set our own romantic standards, and when it comes to the institution of marriage, we get to bust up that church and rebuild it brick by brick until it's a castle of our own design.

The only downside to our charmed lives as single women is the lovingly relentless shit we catch from our mothers as they become increasingly desperate for grandchildren. Back in their day, the only thing more conspicuous than a single lady in her late twenties was one with tattoos. Come over to my place for Thanksgiving dinner, and my mother will happily share with you her theory that the blatant husbandlessness of every woman born in the eighties is directly attributable to the tramp stamp.

That's okay, though. Our moms mean well, and an occasional awkward moment over the holidays is a small price to pay for not having to take any of this husband stuff too seriously.

We've been around the block, and we all know better than to buy what the fairy tales and family sitcoms are selling. We aren't silly schoolgirls dreaming of soul mates. We never expected a Prince Charming, and we're not waiting to be swept off our feet.

Hell, all we really want is a partner in crime. We want our intellectual and emotional equal. We want the alternative to that shirt-stained oafish mess of a man-child pop culture insists on portraying as the standard-issue husband. We have more respect for men than that.

In fact, we love men. Everything about them. They are warm and delicious creatures that make us laugh, carry in the heavy stuff from the car, and on the really good days, bend us over the furniture and fuck us silly.

I've had plenty of men in my time. I've even fallen in love with a few, but as wonderful as a good man can be, I've still yet to meet one I'd be willing to call my husband. Of course, that hasn't stopped the boys from trying. So far, I've turned down four marriage proposals.

The first was from my high school sweetheart. We were just puppies, and he figured that getting down on one knee after a trip to the jewelry store at the mall would be enough to keep me from moving away to Los Angeles. As much as I loved him, he figured wrong.

My second proposal came from a lawyer. We were a filthy hot power couple—two yuppie assholes who spent our early twenties raising hell together in all the darkest corners of Hollywood. The last thing he needed was a wife, and I told him that if he ever proposed, I would turn him down. He didn't believe me until it was too late.

The third man to buy me a ring was a movie producer. What can I say? For a while there, I had a thing for older Jewish men. He was twice my age, and everything about our relationship was an inappropriate cliché, right down to our bondage- and S&M-filled sex life. He did his damnedest to make me his second trophy wife, but there's not a rock at Harry Winston big enough to turn me into a kept woman.

The most recent guy to bend his knee was a doctor. We were never really a couple, not officially. We were best friends for many years, and we loved each other dearly. Still, neither of us was ever in love. He must have dated half the gold-diggers in Beverly Hills before coming out the other end of his mid-life crisis emotionally exhausted. I thought he was joking the night he proposed, but he wasn't. Apparently, I was the least batshit woman in his little black book, and that was enough for him. Honored though I was, it didn't take long to convince him that friendship and sanity weren't quite enough to justify getting married.

Looking back over each of my proposals, I'm happy to say that I don't have any regrets. If given the chance, I'd tell them no all over again. None of those marriages would have lasted more than a few years, and it's so much better to be an ex-girlfriend than it is to be an ex-wife. I'm still close friends with all four of my former suitors, because they all eventually came to realize what I had known all along: a marriage will not fix a relationship. It's not a gilded cage or a consolation prize, and it will not change who we are.

This book may be for the man who might eventually get me to say yes, but I still owe a gracious nod to the men I once had to turn down. Hell, I even owe some begrudging respect to the men who've broken my heart. Yes, there have been a few.

The last time I was in love with a man he broke up with me out of the blue one morning while I was still butt-ass naked. I woke up, walked into the kitchen wearing nothing but a hangover, and found him flipping through a book of old *Far Side* cartoons. He looked up at me and simply said, "I can't do this anymore."

It was without a doubt the most exposed I've ever felt in my entire life, both physically and emotionally. All I could think was, "Are you kidding me? Fucking *Far Side* cartoons?" It wasn't an easy thing to get over, but still, I welcome heartbreak as an inevitability, both the breaking and being broken.

It's the reason I've learned so much from all of my past relationships. I've learned that tomorrow is promised to no one, but that's no reason to talk yourself out of happiness today. I've learned that you can't build a lifelong commitment on outward appearances or infatuation or money. I've learned that there's no such thing as "the one," and when it comes to picking a future husband, I've learned it's the little things that matter.

That's what this book is, really, just a collection of the little things. It's a smirking nod to all the tidbits and minutiae about the men in our lives that make us swoon and then roll our eyes. Every last one of us could fill a book with notes to the men we might one day marry. Who knows? Maybe one day I'll find a man cool enough to call my future husband.

If that ever happens, my notes will be waiting for him.

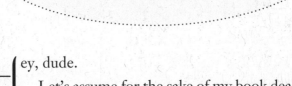

*H*ey, dude.

Let's assume for the sake of my book deal that you do exist. Let's also assume that you're not Ryan Gosling or Tom Brady (this isn't an exercise in fantasy).

My evil genius plan with this little project is that one sunny afternoon in the weeks leading up to our wedding, I will drive you to the nearest bookstore (I hope they still exist in the future), pull a copy of this thing off the shelf, and hand it to you.

If that's what's happening right now, don't get all excited. Yeah, yeah. I wrote a book for you. Big deal. People write books every day. Don't let it go to your head. The important thing for you to do right now is focus, because you've got some homework to do.

I need you to read this book from cover to cover. Trust me, it's more than just a pile of silly notes. It's a cheat sheet, a reference guide to our happily ever after. Study it. Learn it. Memorize it. Use a highlighter if necessary because there's gonna be a quiz, and it's 'til death do us part.

Don't worry. You'll do fine. I wouldn't have said yes to just *anyone*. Just remember, when in doubt, never take any of this marriage stuff too seriously.

Let's go have some fun.

NOTES ON OUR WEDDING

Hey, dude.

If we've come this far, it means that I'm no longer content referring to you as my "spousal equivalent" at cocktail parties. That's a pretty big deal, but before we get to call each other husband and wife without that pesky asterisk next to our relationship status, we have to gather together all of our friends and relatives and make them dance in uncomfortable shoes.

Relax. I'm one of the cool ones. I don't give a shit about the wedding. Walking down the aisle was never a fantasy of mine, and I was never one of those girls who went glassy-eyed while dreaming about her big day. It's not that I don't care. It's just that I've been a maid of honor enough times to know that weddings are a cauldron of stress and family politics. My priorities are a bit different than your average bride's. I just want to throw a massive party where everyone can get hammered for free.

With that in mind, here are a few notes on our wedding.

The Ring

I know you're gonna think I'm crazy, but I don't want a big sparkling whore trophy. Instead of a diamond, how about we travel the world together or start a college fund for our kids?

The Proposal

Clearly you knew better than to make a public spectacle of asking to marry me, or I would have said no just to fuck with you on general principle.

Obey

That word will be conspicuously

missing from our wedding vows.

The Bachelor/ Bachelorette Parties

They're the only time I agree with

policies of "separate but equal"

and "don't ask, don't tell."

Prenup

Hell yes, we got one. Just because we're in love doesn't mean we're gonna make shitty legal and financial decisions.

Screw the Gift Registries

We'll find a clever way to let everyone know we'd prefer cold hard cash.

The Rehearsal Dinner

Do you think the In-N-Out truck

could swing by our hotel?

A Wedding Planner

Whatever.

I have plenty of gay friends.

One Night Only

Wouldn't it be cool if our wedding invitations looked like vintage concert posters?

Doctor of Divinity

I wish Hunter S. Thompson was still around so he could officiate our wedding.

The Wedding Photographer

I wouldn't be opposed to hiring
Michel Gondry or Jonas Akerlund
to shoot the whole wedding as a
whacked-out music video.

The Cake

I'd like to have red velvet cake at the wedding, so unless you want us to look like a couple of murder victims, let's not do the whole "smash it in each other's faces" thing.

Bridesmaids

Mine will be hot.

Their dresses will be, too.

Bad Luck

You're not supposed to see me

on our wedding day until

I walk down the aisle. I guess

that means you'll have to

fuck me wearing a blindfold

that morning.

Open Seating

I think it's ridiculous that people stress out about the protocol and politics of the seating charts at their wedding reception. Ours is gonna be like Southwest Airlines. First come, first served.

The Wedding Dress

I know better than to pick the one that Stephanie Seymour wore in the Guns N' Roses "November Rain" video, but that doesn't mean I don't secretly want it.

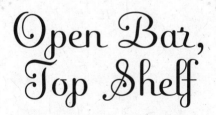

Open Bar, Top Shelf

That's just how we roll.

The DJ

Do you think Skrillex would play a wedding? Do you think our grandmothers would appreciate a good bass drop? Probably not, but I think we should at least try and find out.

The Bouquet

I don't want to throw my bouquet over my shoulder. I want to launch it into the sky like a clay pigeon and let the bridesmaids shoot at it with shotguns.

The Reception

If I choose "Butterfly Kisses"
for the father/daughter dance
portion of our wedding reception,
consider it a cry for help.

Surnames

You keep yours. I keep mine.
Fuck hyphens. If we ever have
kids, we can flip for it.

Hot Damn

You look good in a tux.

Plane Tickets

I'm not saying we gotta have our wedding in Cabo, but a destination wedding is the perfect way to make sure that only our favorite people show up.

Something Old, Something New, Something Borrowed, Something Blue

Just so you know, buying me a pair of fake tits before the wedding would qualify as all four.

The Church

I'd rather not get married in a church, but if your Catholic grandparents put a gun to my head, I would choose the Chapel of the Holy Cross in Sedona just for the architecture.

Elopement

If you want to run off and get married without telling anyone, I'm totally down. It can't be Vegas, though. That's a tacky cliché. It'd have to be somewhere awesome and bizarre, like Machu Picchu.

Let's Write Our Own Vows

This is our marriage, on our terms, for better for worse, for richer for poorer, and even in sickness and in health. If the whole "until death do us part" thing freaks us out, let's stick an asterisk in there. We can change the word "death" to "fate." Let's make whatever promises to each other we're willing to keep, and if the sky falls, so be it.

Hey, dude.

You've met my work friends. You've met my cocktail party friends. You've probably even met a few of my exes, and no doubt you can hang with them all. We both came to the table with fully intact social lives, and it should stay that way.

Keep your friends, all of them. Hang out with them. Go on weekend trips with them. Seriously, I need time with my girls. We'll do just enough co-mingling of our inner circles to keep things interesting. With any luck, your best friend is dating someone cool I don't mind inviting to brunch, and you won't mind having the occasional beer with my best friend's husband.

Here are a few notes on our friends.

{ Never Ask

which one of your friends

I find most attractive.

I have an answer. }

Exes

We both have them, and we can both

be friendly, but let's not pretend

that they're our friends.

My BFF

If you never had a sister, guess what?
You do now.

Keep Your Friends Close,

but don't keep your enemies
closer. In fact, don't bother
keeping enemies at all. Life's too
short for that kind of nonsense.

Ride or Die Bitches

If one of your friends breaks up with a girl I think is awesome, don't for one second expect me to stop hanging out with her. Cool girls are worth their weight in gold.

The Frie-nup

Just so you know, I've got a running list
of the friends I'd keep in the divorce. It
won't hold up in court, but then again,
it wouldn't have to.

Facebook

Our online relationship status
never meant anything to us,
and it never will.

My Girlfriends

Treat mine well. They know more about you than you could possibly imagine.

Your Girlfriends

Have all the female friends you want, but if some floozy tries to hijack your heart, don't think I won't cut a bitch.

Girl's Night Out

For the record, we talk about you a lot *less* than you think, and we get hit on a lot *more* than you think.

Guy's Night Out

Have fun. Feel free to drunk dial me, and always know: I've got bail money on standby.

Smack Talk

Take it as a compliment when my girls start giving you shit. It means they like you. Feel free to give as good as you get.

Flirting

It's never innocent, but then again, neither are we. Let's flirt all we want.

Strip Clubs

Going to a strip club is not cheating.
You do not have to call me to check in.
Have a blast at your college roommate's
bachelor party, and remember to tip well.

Threesomes

Don't ever ask if I'll have a threesome
with one of our friends. Threesomes
are for super-hot strangers we'll
never meet again.

Foursomes and Moresomes

If you wanna start swinging, we'll need to get ourselves a completely separate group of friends for that sort of thing. Trust me on this.

Jealousy

Jealousy is for couples with underlying trust issues. That's just not our style.

My Brunching Crew

This is a sacred group of my inner circle.

Your friends will be vetted thoroughly

before joining us for Bloody Marys.

Circles of Friends

I have many, and they rarely overlap.

You're probably the only person

who'll get to meet them all.

Guy Code

I know it exists, and I respect it, but if I ever hear you uttering the phrase "bros before hos," you're fired from life.

Girl Code

Sorry, dude. If we break up one day, none of my friends will ever date you.

Step Up

If your friends are better dancers than you, I'll be off dancing with them.

That One Friend

Keep him out of our bathroom, please.

House Guests

I've got friends all over the world, and whenever they're in town, our house is their house, and they can stay as long as they like. No complaints, because we'll always have standing invitations to my friends' apartments in Paris and beach houses in Belize.

Chaos Magnets

Life's too short to put up with walking Lifetime movie-of-the-week clichés. If you've got any whacked-out friends who savor drama and thrive on chaos, just cut them the hell out of your life.

Frenemies

I used to have a bunch of them,
but then I realized how toxic it was.
Life is so much better now that I only
surround myself with healthy, happy,
and reliable friends.

Birth Control

Condoms are 98 percent
effective, but I still say the best
form of birth control is visiting
our friends with small children.

NOTES ON FAMILY

Hey, dude.

My family is crazy. Your family is crazy. Everybody's family is fucking crazy. That's just the way it is, but hey, we've got each other's back during the holidays. I should warn you ahead of time that my grandparents are a little bit racist, but don't worry. It's in a hilarious way. Also, thanks ahead of time for calming me down when my mother starts getting passive-aggressive about her lack of grandkids.

Speaking of which, I guess since you're going to be my husband one day, that sort of implies that I'm down to start a family with you. That's big, scary stuff. You should know by now that I'm a little freaked out about nine months of pregnancy, and I'm absolutely terrified at the notion of squeezing tiny, screaming people out of my vagina. Also, I have a tendency to call babies "it." I'm sure that with enough oxytocin coursing through my bloodstream, I won't do that to our kids.

Anyway, here are a few notes on family.

{ Relax

I will not turn into my mother. }

Sibling Rivalry

If I'm in a fight with my sister, don't take my side. Don't take her side. Don't try to play peacemaker or devil's advocate. Just get the hell out of the way.

Daddy

I don't call my father that.

I'm sure as hell not calling you that.

My Family Gatherings

I will point out the heavy drinkers and

cousins with weed upon our arrival.

After that, I won't listen to complaints

of boredom.

Your Family Gatherings

If you can't find me, check with the heavy drinkers and cousins with weed.

Family Politics

My parents are die-hard *Fox News*–flavored Republicans. Sorry. Just smile and nod when they start talking politics. Whatever you do, don't engage.

Thanksgiving and Christmas

You will have to schlep across the country with me for at least one of these holidays every year for the rest of our natural lives. They will be big. They will be loud. They will be exhausting.

Slightly Racist Grandparents

I have a working theory during the holidays that the number of times my Nana will make an inappropriate reference to someone's ethnicity is in direct proportion to the number of lipstick stains she leaves on her wine glass.

Google

My mom figured out how to
use the Internet, so your name
better come up clean.

In-Laws

Don't worry. Your parents
are gonna love me.

Mazel Mazel

If you're Jewish, I promise your mother will eventually get over the fact that I'm not.

Before Knocking Me Up,

just know, if I don't get to drink or do drugs for nine months, then you don't get to drink or do drugs for nine months.

Artificial Insemination

If it comes to this, please don't complain about having to jerk off into a cup. I'm the one who has to take a turkey baster up my cooch.

"We"

"We" are not pregnant. "I" am pregnant. Saying that "we" are pregnant when I'm the one carrying the baby is like you eating a five-pound burrito and then claiming that "we" have gas.

Natural Childbirth

Nope, it's not gonna happen. Don't even suggest it. When I give birth, I want all the drugs.

The Delivery Room

Please, no peeking behind the curtain.
I'd like to get laid again.

The Bidet

Our children will know better than
to use it as a drinking fountain.

We're Gonna Make a Lot of Parenting Mistakes.

Let's not make putting leashes

on our children when we go

to the mall one of them.

If I ever start a sentence with "If you were my dad..."

Immediately tell me to shut the hell up.

Sticky Fingers

That toddler that smells like syrup is not touching my iPhone. I don't care if it's our kid.

Teenagers

Let's fight the urge to shelter our kids by taking the time to remember how much we had already figured out by their age.

Legacy Naming

Tell your Uncle Bart that we love him very much, but we're not naming our kid anything that rhymes with fart.

Oops!

If our kids ever walk in on us while we're having sex, don't freak out. We can just tell them that we're wrestling. Of course, Mommy will be winning.

Citizens of the World

Our kids will speak multiple languages. They will have passports before they have driver's licenses. They will be cooler than us.

The Grow Up Plan from Gerber Life

I know, it's for our future children, but I kinda want to sign myself up, too.

Special Snowflake Syndrome

We'll teach our kids that they are capable, not special. The world has too many narcissists.

My Mom and Dad

They can be a handful, but they were amazing parents. We'd be lucky to raise kids half as well as they did. One of the most important lessons I learned from them is that good parenting is a constant exercise in showing our kids their dignity.

NOTES FROM OUR HOME

Hey, dude.

If I've agreed to marry you, that means we're probably already living together. That's a good thing. We should both know what we're getting ourselves into.

I am wild, which by definition means that I am not domesticated. When it comes to our home, you should know that while I might be a neat freak, you are not marrying Martha Stewart. I won't let you get away with leaving dishes in the sink, I only use a Swiffer for procrastination purposes, and the only reason I'd ever fold your underwear is so I can throw away the pairs that have holes in them. In other words, our home will be clean, but I won't be cleaning up after you.

Don't worry. I'll chip in for the maid service. Fair is fair.

Here are a few notes from our home.

One-Ply Toilet Paper

Are you nuts? Take that shit back—I'm not wiping my ass with sandpaper just because it was on sale.

Cleaning

Cleaning the bathroom does not mean pee-blasting the shit stains off the back of the toilet bowl.

Boundaries

It will never be okay for you to leave the door open while you take a shit.

Coasters and Condoms

You didn't think just because we got married you'd have to stop using them, did you? Do I need to remind you of the damage fluids can do?

My Side of the Bed

is whichever one doesn't

have the wet spot.

Alarm Clocks

If you insist on setting that shit to go

off an hour before we have to get up,

I will smack your dick like it's

the snooze button.

Carpentry

I'm not going to assume that you know how to assemble or fix things any better than I can. If it takes more than a screwdriver and a hammer, let's leave it to the professionals.

Climate Control

Don't you dare touch that fucking thermostat! I am a delicate flower and you pee on trees. Adapt.

The Coffee Table

That shit is for Taschen and
Tom Ford books, not your feet.

Deuce

Go drop one in the guest bathroom.

I'm putting on my makeup in here.

The Grill

Okay, I get it. Lighting the grill is your thing. You can be the one to do it.

Hot Water

It's a precious resource. We can have shower sex, but you gotta let me finish washing my hair.

Incense

Are you a monk? Do you play the fucking sitar? Don't light that shit around me.

Dirty Laundry

I will pretend that the skid marks in your boxer briefs are a sign that we've achieved ultimate intimacy, and you can pretend that my period stains are Rorschach tests.

{ The Lawn }

It's not gonna mow itself.

Man Cave

If we can afford a home with a den, it's all yours. I'll take the drawing room. I don't draw, and you're not a bear, but we need our own space to get drunk and watch porn.

Oompa Loompas

Can we get, like, three of them?

Pretty please!

Tampons

You'll have to buy them for me on occasion, but I promise, you'll never have to see the string.

Pants

There is no good reason to wear them around the house unless one of us is frying bacon.

Spiders

Don't you kill that spider!
Here, let me catch him and
put him outside.

Toilet Paper

The roll goes over. Never under.
Don't act like you've never stayed
in a nice hotel.

A Vacuum Cleaner?

Just to be clear, if you buy me
something that plugs into the wall,
it doesn't count as a gift.

Diet Coke

Not Coke, Pepsi, Coke Zero,
or fucking Diet Dr. Pepper.
And if you take the last one
out of the fridge, we're gonna
have problems. *Big* problems.

Relocating

I don't care how much money they're
offering you, we're not moving to
New Jersey.

I Don't Love Martha Stewart Because She's a Homemaker.

I love Martha Stewart because she's a hardcore bitch who runs a media empire.

If You Don't Flush After Using the Toilet,

I'm allowed to use your beard trimmer

to touch up my landing strip.

NOTES ON FOOD

Hey, dude.

They say the way to a man's heart is through his stomach, and while I'm confident I know a number of alternate routes, there's something to be said for a good homemade sauce.

So yeah, you lucked out. You're gonna eat well around me. I love to cook, and some of my dirtiest secrets are recipes. Hell, I'll even make you a sandwich after sex. (Not every time, but often enough that you can tell your friends.) Of course, I know how to make reservations, too. Be prepared to wine and dine me, and yes, I like restaurants with Michelin stars. (Not every time, but often enough that I can tell my friends.)

We're gonna spend a lot of time chowing down together, so as long as you have table manners and are willing to try new things, we'll get along just fine.

Here are a few notes on food.

Cold Cuts

If we have ham and you leave less than three slices in the package, you should just stab me in my sleep. What am I supposed to do with less than three pieces of ham? Dry my tears?

No

I'm not finished with that
(but you can have a bite).

A Sandwich

Fuck yeah, I'll make you one.

If You Aren't Willing to Smell the Milk,

then obviously I'm not

willing to smell the milk.

Just fucking toss it.

Bacon

Bring home the bacon. Literally. I love bacon. That shit is delicious.

Doing the Dishes

If I cook, you do the dishes. If you cook, I do the dishes. That's the way we'll do it until I pop out a couple of sous chefs.

Ethnic Food

You can dislike something only after you have tried it. There will be no food bigots in our home.

Bolognese

If you can make a sauce from scratch, your entire prep time will be comprised of me wanting to fuck you.

Bourbon-Soaked Banana Cake

It's not a dessert. It's a culinary
metaphor for our relationship.

A Burrito

I'm always down for one.
You don't even have to ask.

Condiments

We do not live at the
ball park or the county fair.
Do not bring plain yellow
mustard into our home.

Magic Brownies

Before diving into a plate of my
homemade baked goods, double
check that they aren't medicinal.

Meat Loaf

It's a recipe, not a musician.

Culinary Sophistication

You know the difference between Anthony Bourdain and Rachael Ray.

The Food Network

I'm cool with Giada De Laurentiis

being on your celebrity sex list,

as long as you're cool with her

being on mine.

Nutella

Is it weird that I have a recurring sex dream where your cum tastes like Nutella?

Waffles and Ice Cream

Yeah, that's what I want for breakfast. You got a problem with that?

White Zinfandel

You know that's not rosé, right?

Grilled Cheese Night

Whether it's artisanal gruyere and prosciutto or Kraft singles and bologna slices, you can't go wrong on grilled cheese night.

Sushi

Please don't be the numnard who orders chicken teriyaki and a fork at the Japanese restaurant.

Pizza Toppings

Go nuts. Balls to the wall.

The pie is our canvas.

Stuffing Your Face

I love a steak. You love a steak. That's no excuse to partake in some tacky restaurant's steak challenge. I refuse to sit by and watch you eat 72 ounces of anything.

Starbucks Compatibility

I am not a grande skinny caramel macchiato and you are not a venti chai latte half-and-half. We are both just plain fucking coffee, one cream, one sugar.

Rexing

I am not one of those girls who
willingly goes without chowing down.
If I haven't eaten all day, you'll be
able to tell. Don't ask me why
I'm behaving erratically, just put
a slice in my mouth.

Vanilla

That's our ice cream,
not our sex life.

Diet Coke and Pinot Grigio

They are my lifeblood, and I will always order them together. Sure, it's tacky, but unless the restaurant has a Michelin star, that's just how I roll.

The Usual

If my hangover reaches level four, which is Indian delivery, you better know that when I say "Green stuff, red stuff, the drink," I mean saag paneer, chicken tikka masala, and a mango lassi. Garlic naan should be an unspoken understanding between us.

Midnight Snacks

It's late. You're hungry. Feel free to climb out of bed and raid the fridge, but hurry back, because I guarantee you're not gonna find anything as delicious as my pussy.

NOTES ON FUCKING

$\mathcal{H}$ey, dude.

    I love sex. Always have. Always will. I had lots of it before I met you, and now that we're together, I plan on having lots more. Almost all of it is gonna be with you.

    That's right. I said almost.

    I don't mean to freak you out or anything, but I'm not all that monogamous. Don't worry, I'll never cheat on you, but fidelity and monogamy aren't the same thing. Being true and faithful in a relationship has no inherent connection to how many sexual partners you have. Lust isn't love. Flirting isn't intimacy. Sex isn't passion. As long as we keep the love, intimacy, and passion to ourselves, I have absolutely no problem if we share a little lust, flirting, and sex with a few other lucky and well-chosen partners over the years.

Yes, that means we can have a threesome.

Oh, and I suppose we should get this out of the way now. Yes, your cock is huge. No, it's not the biggest I've ever seen, but it's still quite impressive. It's perfect, really. Now please stop asking me about it, and here are a few more notes on our sex life.

Breakfast in Bed

will be how you refer to going
down on me in the morning.

Our History

There is no use pretending that we've
never been around the block. We
both know that our sexual skills were
built with years of slutty practice and
morally questionable decisions.

Backrubs or Blowjobs

I'm ridiculously good at both, but you can only pick one. Sorry, dude. You can't have it all on the same day. That's too much transcendent pleasure for one man to handle. I'll spoil you, but I won't spoil you rotten.

Batteries

If I ever have to steal the batteries

from your remote control to use in

my vibrator, you should probably

take the hint.

Chafing

Don't worry, babe. I promise

to spit before I shine.

Daylight Savings

I don't care if we lost an hour.

We're still having morning sex.

Fantasies

Yours will not have anything

to do with football.

Faking

I won't fake orgasms with you.

If you get me off, you'll know.

If you don't, you'll know.

Hate Fuck

It's the only excuse for

going to bed angry.

Choke Me

Just enough, babe.

Honorable Discharge

I'll understand if it was an accident, but if you cum in my eye on purpose, I'm retaliating with hot sauce.

Oral

Four out of five dentists recommend going down on me every day.

Wienering

Workday sexting can be a fun distraction, but please don't send me pictures of your penis unless you've done something funny like put a doughnut around it.

Period Sex

I know you don't care,

but these are Frette sheets.

Get a beach towel.

Sharing

If both of us have herpes, it's kind of

like neither of us has herpes.

Queefs

Yeah, they're hilarious.

Glad my vagina could provide

some postcoital comic relief.

Role Play

Let's reenact that one scene from
Blue Valentine. Not the beginning
or the end, just the whole "you going
down on me" part. If all goes well,
we can reenact the last scene
from *Brown Bunny*.

Vertigo

Can you put me right-side up now?

This position is making me dizzy.

You Do Not Have to Spoon Me.

It's hot, and my arm is asleep. Let's call it even, and I'll see you in the morning.

Don't Stop

if I walk in on
you masturbating.

Orgasms

I'm responsible for mine.

You're responsible for yours.

It's not a competition, and it's

sure as hell not a race.

Victoria's Secret

The secret is that bitch makes shitty underwear.

Public Displays of Affection

I'll never be cool with you being all kissy-face with me in front of other people, but if you want to sneak off and fuck in a spot where we might get caught, I'm totally down.

Fingerblasting

Please wash your hands after handling jalepeños. Nothing kills the mood quicker than me screaming in agony, running to the freezer, and spending the next half hour with ice cubes up my snatch.

The Best Way

The best way to keep me from making love to you is to refer to the act of fucking as "making love."

Underwear

If I'm seducing you and my underwear is anything other than cotton, pretend it's awesome. Even if it has arbitrary bows you don't understand, for the sake of your blowjob, humor me.

Proper Technique

There's something about tying my hair back before giving you a blowjob that makes me feel like a fucking samurai.

NOTES ON FUCKING UP

$\mathcal{H}$ey, dude.

As much as we love each other, it can't all be wine and roses. We're gonna fight. All couples do. The problem is, I'm really good at it. I have an arsenal of mind games that would make Machiavelli weep, and when you cross the line, I'm not afraid to go nuclear.

Sometimes you're gonna piss me off, and inevitably there will be nights when you'll end up sleeping on the sofa. Neither of us wants that, so I need you to really focus here. This may be the most important part of the book, because if you pay attention, you will save yourself endless buckets of grief.

Consider this chapter a map through a mine field. Trust me, I'm giving you pure gold here.

Here are a few notes on fucking up.

When in Doubt,

shut the fuck up.

Apologies

You have to be able to give them

without using the word "sorry."

Of course you're sorry. So what?

If you can't tell me what you're

sorry for, it doesn't count.

Cheating

If you willfully participate or conspire to participate in an act of intimacy with the foreknowledge that I would reasonably consider that act to be a breach of the mutually understood and agreed upon terms of our relationship, that is cheating.

Princess

Don't ever fucking
call me that.

Your Word

Keep that shit. Always. There's no
quicker way for me to lose respect for
someone than not keeping your word.

Don't Cheat

There will be hell to pay.

Anger Management

Yelling and screaming has its

place every once in a while, but if

you ever lay a hand on me in anger,

I promise you will find out what

it's like to spend the

night in jail.

Irreconcilable Differences

If you develop a sudden interest in *Two and a Half Men*, we'll have to reevaluate our marriage.

Fair Warning

If I've seen you lie to other people, I'll know when you lie to me.

Projection

If you think I'll ever let you get away with making me feel bad about your own insecurities, your ego has another thing coming.

Astrology

The alignment of the stars has nothing to do with why you're sometimes an asshole.

Apples and Oranges

Feel free to check out other women's tits, but if you start comparing them to mine, you're gonna be in big trouble.

I Gotta Be Honest

Don't use the phrase "I gotta be honest." It usually means that you're lying and that you're about to be an asshole.

Is There an iPhone App That Makes a Rattlesnake Sound?

Would that be enough of a hint that you're about to fuck up?

Bullshit

If you tell me I look beautiful when I know I look like absolute shit, I will not cry sparkly tears of love and joy. I will know you are a liar.

{ Whiskey Dick }

Never get too drunk to fuck.

I Knew I Loved You Before I Met You.

Shut the fuck up. No, you didn't.

And if you ever quote Savage Garden

again, I'm filing for divorce.

Wrong Hole

Come on, dude.

Please, Let Me Pull the Stick out of Your Ass.

I'll light it like a torch and use it to show you the way.

Lotion

Did you use my Créme de la Mer moisturizer to jerk off? You idiot. That shit costs more per ounce than Vegas cocaine. If you run out of Jergens, use spit next time.

Name Calling

No name calling during fights unless the names are hilarious enough to distract us from why we're fighting. Might I suggest thundercunt or cockgobbler?

A Gym Membership

is not a gift. If you decide to "surprise" me with one, I'll know you think I'm fat, and I'll retaliate by surprising you with a Viagra prescription.

Crossing the Line

There are certain things you can say that you can never take back. You'll know it when it happens. Be prepared for the consequences.

Flowers are Lovely, but I Prefer Books.

Please keep that in mind next time you fuck up.

Orgasms Are Always Better Than Generic Compliments.

Something else to remember

the next time you fuck up.

Go Ahead. Ask Siri How to Change a Flat Tire.

I will never let you forget this moment for as long as we both shall live.

NOTES ON YOUR APPEARANCE

Hey, dude.

You're hot. Every time I see you, I want to break off a piece. Of course, I say that now because you're my future husband, but that's not gonna last forever. Beauty fades. Yours. Mine. Everyone's. The good news is, style is forever, and I'm gonna make sure you have some.

You're gonna learn how to rock a tailored suit before you start graying at the temples, and in the meantime, I'm gonna teach you how an adult male should dress. Don't be surprised when some of your old, ratty clothes start disappearing from your closet. That's right, I threw them out. They had to go. Deal with it.

Grooming is also key, and while I don't expect you

to start coming with me to the manicurist, I won't mind if you start using a little of my moisturizer. I promise, I'm gonna keep you looking sharp. I wouldn't have it any other way.

Here are a few notes on your appearance.

We Are Not Birds.

I will be the decorative one. Your jewelry collection should be 95 percent smaller than mine.

{ Ed Hardy Anything }

Over my dead body.

Your Beard

Trim, don't shave.

Your Pubes

Like I said, trim, don't shave.

Zits

I will pop your back zits if you
ask me to, but I won't enjoy it.

Ascots

That shit doesn't fly
unless you're British.

Bedazzler

You are not a cast member on
Jersey Shore. The only things on
your shirt that are allowed to
sparkle are the cufflinks.

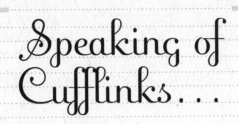

Speaking of Cufflinks...

Let's start your collection.

Big Boy Pants

If you're going to wear sweats to the restaurant, I'm telling the hostess to bring you some crayons and a cartoon placemat.

Foot Calluses

Fred Flintstone has an excuse. You don't. Go get a pedicure immediately.

Is That Axe Body Spray?

You are dead to me.

Cleavage

You're not allowed to have more than me. Your shirts have buttons for a reason, and absolutely no deep V's, under any circumstances.

True Religion

You can stop looking for those jeans you used to wear with the embroidered dragon because I burned them. That kind of douche-baggery is not acceptable.

Goatee

Are you taking me to your
gallery opening tonight? I didn't
think so. Shave that thing.

Uncut

should only apply to cocaine and
cult movies. Honestly, I'd rather
you were circumcised.

Cobwebs

Better not become a nickname
for your pubes.

T-Shirts

They're fine as a layering item, but please don't let yourself become a walking bumper sticker. Remember, there have never been words screen-printed on a T-shirt clever enough to outweigh how tacky that shit looks on a grown-ass man.

{ Pink }

Wear it.

Cool Socks

I love it when a man has on something more creative than Gold Toes when we kick off our shoes. It's an attention-to-detail thing, and I'll make sure you have a whole drawer full.

Get Yourself at Least One Bespoke Suit.

Trust me, it's all about the fit, and that shit is worth every penny.

Steez

You got it.

Sports Jerseys Are for Athletes.

Unless you're on the team, you shouldn't be wearing one.

Aloha Attire

Come on, dude. No Hawaiian shirts unless we are actually in Hawaii. You don't see me walking around in muumuus, do you?

Grunge Flannel

We all love Nirvana and Pearl Jam, but unless you and I move to Portland, you've got no excuse to dress like this. The rule of thumb in recycled trends is that if you are old enough to have worn it the first time, you shouldn't wear it when it comes back around.

Silk Ties

I promise not to use your favorite ones for bondage.

Time to Clean Out Your Closet?

If you don't like it, if it doesn't fit you, if it needs repair, if it doesn't look good on you...get rid of it!

Clip-Ons Are for Children.

Men know how to tie a proper bowtie, so figure it out. It's not all that difficult, and at the end of the evening, you'll get to undo the knot and let it hang down your collar like you're one of the Rat Pack. That shit makes me weak in the knees.

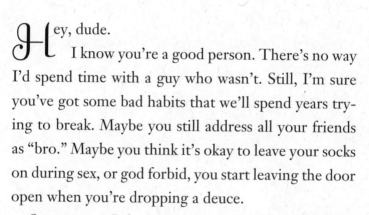

NOTES ON YOUR BEHAVIOR

Hey, dude.

I know you're a good person. There's no way I'd spend time with a guy who wasn't. Still, I'm sure you've got some bad habits that we'll spend years trying to break. Maybe you still address all your friends as "bro." Maybe you think it's okay to leave your socks on during sex, or god forbid, you start leaving the door open when you're dropping a deuce.

Sorry, man. I don't care how comfortable we get with each other. Certain things will never be appropriate. Don't worry, I'll get you acting right. Just remember, it's not nagging. It's training.

Here are a few notes on your behavior:

Table Manners

You already know the basics,
or we wouldn't have made it
past the first date.

Biceps

I love that you have them, but don't
ever offer me a ticket to the gun show.

Farts Are Hilarious.

There's no use pretending otherwise. Still, if you ever attempt a Dutch Oven while we're in bed together, I promise, your butthole will regret it.

Fixing Shit

I'm not going to automatically assume that you're super handy, but if you happen to know your way around a toolbox, it's gonna make me want to break something just to watch you fix it.

Attention

Undivide that shit and give it to me.

Pretentious Buzzwords

We do not have "synergy." We are not "interfacing." We never use the word "concierge" as an adjective or the word "creative" as a noun.

Acquiesce

Not only do you know how to spell it, you know what it means and how to do it.

Pedestals

I don't want you to put me on one
or bend over backward for me.
I may, however, ask you to bend
me over a pedestal. That sounds
like a fucking blast.

Head Scratches

Dude, why don't you moan
like that when we're fucking?

Adulthood

When the Bible said "put away childish things," it was referring specifically to your PlayStation.

Class

It's one of those things you can never have too much of, kinda like toilet paper and lube.

Arcade Fire

You think *The Suburbs* is a great album, not a great lifestyle.

Baby Talk

Never, under any circumstances, ever. No exceptions. Not even to actual babies.

Midlife Crisis

You won't have to buy a hot new convertible because we'll already have one.

Irritable Bowel Syndrome

Don't be a hypochondriac. You just have to fart.

The Hair Fairy

There is no such thing. Clean that disgusting ring of beard shavings out of the sink yourself.

Travel

Even if we're not on the run from the law, if you consistently slow us down at airports or borders, I'll have to cut you loose.

Selfishness Is a Symptom of Immaturity.

Put down the Ayn Rand and pick up some Khalil Gibran.

Procrastination

The longer you wait, the harder it gets. There is only one situation where this works out well.

Tact

Never refer to any sex act as a "servicing." Your penis is not a dipstick.

TiVo

Yes, it makes cute noises, and it knows what television shows you like, but please don't talk to TiVo like it's the family pet.

There Is a Tiny Courtroom Stenographer Living in My Head,

and that bitch is more than happy to read me back the record any time it's necessary. Fair warning: that includes every argument, every promise, and every conversation we've ever had, verbatim.

Proper Introductions

If you don't remember to introduce
me to people at social functions,
I won't remember to keep
standing at your side.

Soul-Searing Eye Contact

Do it right, and it will get you
(almost) anything.

If I Die Young,

feel free to fall in love again and remarry, but if you ever take the bitch to our spot by the bar at Mastro's, I will haunt your ass forever.

Bad Moods

I get it. You're hungry and had a lousy day at work. Go eat a sandwich, then rub one out or something, but don't take that shit out on me. If I wanted to live with an overbearing menopausal woman, I would've married your mother.

NOTES FOR SPECIAL OCCASIONS

Hey, dude.

When it comes to gifts and special occasions, most people say it's the thought that counts. Screw that. Original thought counts. Creativity counts, but what passes for plain old thought these days is usually just a pre-packaged byproduct of corporate marketing.

The only thing I like less than Hallmark holidays are actual Hallmark greeting cards. Those kinds of things are as unappetizing and artificial as processed cheese. Special occasions aren't special when everyone else is doing the exact same thing, especially when no one can even tell you why. I'd much rather celebrate our own special occasions, and if you're going to get me a card, I suggest you find one that's letterpress.

This isn't me being spoiled. This is me having too much self-respect to swallow special occasions that came out of a can. Traditions are much too important for us not to create them ourselves.

Here are a few notes on special occasions.

Birthdays

Absolutely no surprise parties. It'll be in the prenup.

Our Anniversary

Nothing says "I forgot until this morning" like a scented lotion gift set.

Staycation

Let's get a hotel room. I need you to fuck the workweek out of me.

Lingerie

Buying me Agent Provocateur in the wrong size is infinitely better than buying me Victoria's Secret in the right size.

Mardi Gras

No, show *me* your tits.

Oscar Night

If you ever win an Academy Award,

I'll totally let you use it as a sex toy.

Sunday Mornings

I might get down on my knees, but it's

not gonna be to pray.

Valentine's Day

I don't care. No, really. It's a bullshit Hallmark holiday. There's no need for candy, flowers, or anything cheesy. Just get me off that night.

Easter

Let's go on a hunt for eggs that vibrate!

Halloween Fun Fact

Fishnets and chain mail don't mix.

Trick or Treat

I play tricks. You give me treats.

I'm Dreaming of a White Christmas

Not in a racist way or anything.

Black Friday

The only way we'll participate in Black Friday is by starting a death pool with our friends and betting on how many shoppers get trampled.

New Year's Eve

I don't care if we go big or stay home,

as long as we get to make out

at midnight.

Playing Hooky

I'll call out of work

if you call out of work.

Thank-You Notes

You handwrite them, preferably on custom stationery.

{ I Had a Rough Day }

I need a massage.

On my vagina.

Poppin' Bottles

My celebratory champagne of choice is Perrier-Jouët. Why? Effervescence. It has more bubbles, my dear. Keep a bottle on standby at all times.

Throwing Up

You don't have to hold my hair back or anything. Make yourself useful and get me a mint and a fresh drink.

Birthday Blues

When I say I don't want anything and am going to skip celebrating this year, whatever you do, don't believe me.

Gifting Conspiracies

Feel free to plan and plot with my best friend over what to get me for my birthday.

Bar Mitzvahs

Make sure I don't have too much wine at those things, because I have a tendency to start tossing around inappropriate Yiddish words at all the Jewish grandparents.

Baptisms and Christenings

Don't get any of that holy water on me. I might burst into flames.

Super Bowl Sunday

Tom Brady is on television?

Awesome.

Memorial Day

I see this weekend as an opportunity to commemorate all the stupid shit I've done in my life by day-drinking in a bikini.

Other People's Weddings

I've been a bridesmaid nine times. That's it. I'm done. I want to start wearing my own dresses and hanging out with you.

{ Vegas }

You'd better be able to keep up.

NOTES ON DATE NIGHT

ℋey, dude.

You should know I've got a respectable collection of dancin' shoes. If you want to keep me happy, make sure I have a reason to wear them as often as possible. You see, I had what might be called an "active" social life before you met me. I may have swapped out most of my late-night partying hours for late-night cuddling with you, but that doesn't mean I don't still have the need to blow the roof off a joint every now and again.

It doesn't have to be every weekend, but I'll need stamps on my wrist and ringing in my ears at least a couple times a month or else I'll start climbing the walls. Come on, let's go have some fun!

Here are a few notes on date night.

Chivalry

For the record, that shit goes both ways. You hold the door for me, and I let you eat off my plate.

Third Wheels

Sure, we can grab dinner and drinks with your buddy who's feeling a bit lonely, but that doesn't count as date night.

Movie Theater Make-Out Sessions

If we get bored in the theater, I'll totally let you fingerblast me like we're teenagers with a curfew. (Don't start picking boring movies on purpose, though.)

Art Museums

We're going. Deal with it. Pretend
you're Ferris Bueller or something.

Bamboozled

If you get me all excited about a fancy
party in the hills and it turns out to be
a bunch of your buddies playing video
games, you can find your own way home.

{ Game Night }

Might I suggest naked
Crisco Twister?

Amuse-Bouche

Just say the word, and I can be back
from the ladies room to slip my
underwear in your pocket before the
waiter brings the wine.

Amateur Night

Sorry, we don't qualify.

Karaoke Night

There aren't enough beers in Milwaukee for me to get drunk enough to sing Journey in front of a group of strangers, but you go right ahead.

What a Fool Believes

A fool believes it's okay to attempt singing Michael McDonald on karaoke night. Don't be a fool.

Planning Ahead

Are we having some drinks, or are we havin' some DRANKS? Let me know, so I can wear the appropriate earrings.

Last Call

Close out your tab already. We've got fuckin' to do.

Double Dates

We'll only go on them with our friends who date cool people.

Unbelievable

Did you really think I was gonna let you leave the house wearing that shirt?

Let's Howl Tonight

I'm feeling a bit Ginsbergy in an "angel-headed hipsters burning for the ancient heavenly connection" kind of way.

Valet

Please don't circle the block five times looking for parking when the restaurant has valet.

Are We in a Hurry or Something?

I appreciate you picking up the tab, but please wait until I'm done eating before you ask for the damn check.

Bring the Camera!

Let's go do something tonight that will embarrass our future children.

After-Dinner Cigars

Don't be that guy.

Uncontrollable Laughter

Let's just get baked and have a *Chappelle's Show* marathon.

Moderation in All Things, Including Moderation,

which is why tonight we're doin' hoodrat shit with our friends.

My Guns N' Roses Hoodie

If you come home to find me wearing

it, you might as well just pop some

popcorn, consult my Netflix queue,

and check my TiVo recommendations.

Sorry, dude. I'm in for the evening.

Alpha-Male Behavior

If we're out together and a stranger makes inappropriate sexual advances, please don't hit him. I'd prefer that the two of you work through your disagreement via a freestyle rap battle.

Restaurant Rudeness

No matter how bad the waiter is, we do not make a scene. We speak to the manager, make a graceful exit, and don't let it ruin our evening.

Dinner Parties

We'll never show up without a bottle of wine and a mutually agreed upon safe word.

Have You Seen Frank Sinatra's or David Bowie's Mug Shots?

Their shirt collars were crisp, their suits were unwrinkled, and not a hair on their heads was out of place. That's what those dudes looked like after being arrested, so the least you could do is look that sharp before taking me out for a night on the town.

NOTES ON THE RULES

Hey, dude.

I'm not a big fan of rules. It may seem like sometimes I'm telling you what to do, but I'm not. You're not the boss of me. I'm not the boss of you. Do whatever you want.

That being said, actions have consequences, so instead of thinking of these notes as rules, just think of them as guidelines to our mutual happiness.

You want me to be happy, right? I thought so. Here are a few notes on how to keep me that way.

Angry Birds

make for angry wives. Put that stupid game down and play with me instead.

Bitch

When you call me one, it's a compliment. When I call you one, it's not.

Books

You read them. Ones without pictures.

Camel Toe

You will always let me know
if I'm sporting one.

Cuddle Time

It's mandatory.

The Daily Show

Fuck CNN. We get our evening
news from Jon Stewart.

Double Standards

I get to be bisexual and you don't. You get to fart and I don't. Considering the oppressive gender politics endured by previous generations, I think we can both live with that.

Emoticons

There is no excuse for anyone born in the twentieth century to use them.

Emotional Baggage

Must fit neatly into the
overhead compartment.

Couples Counseling Is for Pussies.

Let's go rob a bank together.

No Cats.
No Way.

If we want to get a pet, let's find a species that's both hypoallergenic and *not* a miniature killing machine constantly plotting our deaths while we sleep.

Jokes

You will know how to tell one and know how to take one.

Nagging

I prefer the term "training." Deal with it.

Internet

Let's not diss each other on it.

Ultimatums

I will always call your bluff.

Write It Down

Just because you've memorized the stats of every player on your fantasy team doesn't mean you'll remember what to get at the grocery store. Make a list and check it twice. Has Santa taught you nothing?

Terms of Endearment

If you insist on using them, please be creative. You should know better than to come at me with "sweetie pie" or "sugar plum." I think "honey cunt" has a nice ring, don't you?

Skymall Appliances

Let's never be one of those couples who gets all excited about the latest Dyson vacuum cleaner, a Sub Zero refrigerator that plays Pandora, or, god forbid, a fucking Margaritaville blender.

Weight Gain

If I get fat, be nice.

It's probably your fault.

Blood

If you'll pay hundreds of dollars for blood splatter seats at a UFC fight, you are not allowed to squirm at the mention of my period.

Gambling

You don't gamble. You take risks.

There's a huge difference.

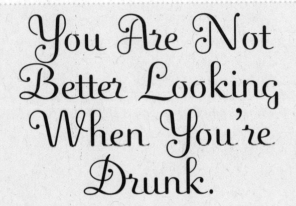

You Are Not Better Looking When You're Drunk.

You're better looking when *I'm* drunk.

Joint Accounts

Keep your own passwords. Keep your own Facebook. Keep your own email. You don't want to see my shoe sale spam, and I don't want to see your porn spam.

Other Women

You will never say stupid shit like, "I may look at the menu, but I'll never order." This is mainly because you are not a tool who objectifies women, but it's also because I like playing with girls, and we'll both get to enjoy that over the years.

NOTES ON ME

Hey, dude.

What can I say about myself? I am a riddle, wrapped in a mystery, inside an enigma, wearing Louboutins, but perhaps there is a key. That key is the fact that I've got a really big heart. Do me a favor and try not to break it, because you could, very easily.

When it comes to the men I love, I share myself honestly and completely. I'm totally vulnerable. That's okay, though. I embrace my vulnerability. I own that shit. I'm proud of it. Emotional honesty is the only way to fly, and as my future husband, I trust you with the good, the bad, and the crazy. With that in mind, I thought I'd hook you up with a list of some of the little things that make me tick.

Here are a few notes on me.

My Ass

Patting it, pinching it, spanking it, biting it, fucking it, and occasionally lighting fires underneath it each have their appropriate moment. Your discretion is key. Use it wisely.

My Tramp Stamp

Aren't you glad I gave you something to aim for back there?

Promiscuity

You know better than to ask how many men I've slept with, and I know better than to have ever kept track.

Shopping at Sephora

Here, take this flare gun. If I'm not back with some lip gloss in twenty minutes, fire it once into the air and cancel all of our credit cards.

Jell-O Shots

Yeah, I can make them firmer than a pair of fake tits. Not all of my college years were wasted.

The Real Housewives

Those whacked out bitches are my reality TV crack. Deal with it.

Robes

Mine is sacred. You are not allowed to borrow it, wash it, or use it as a cum towel. Ever.

Boo, the World's Cutest Dog

Ahhh! I want a Boo dog so badly! Can we get one? Please, please, please!

Shoes

Think of them as the female equivalent
of a blowjob. Really good ones can
make everything better, and
I'll always want more.

Graciousness

If you give me a thoughtful present,
and I forget to say thank you,
call me out on my shit.

Couponing and Cupcakery

If I turn into a lobotomized Jesus freak who gives up my career for our marriage and then starts yammering about this kind of insufferable bullshit, you have my permission to smother me with a pillow like McMurphy at the end of *One Flew Over the Cuckoo's Nest*.

Save Money, Live Worse

I have nothing against big box or discount stores—I love Target, and I'll chainsaw through a TJ Maxx like Rachel Zoe on crack—but please don't ever make me shop at Walmart. That place sucks the life force right out of me.

Quirky Hipster Chick

I will never play kickball or the ukulele.

{ Good Under Pressure. Good in the Sack. }

Yeah, I'm a keeper.

I'll Totally Admit When I'm Wrong,

but don't hold your breath waiting

for that to happen.

The Smell of New Leather Makes Me a Little Bit Horny.

Feel free to use this information

to your advantage.

I'm Not a Deviant.

I'm a sociological trailblazer.

My "Hubby"

I will not refer to you as my "hubby" or anything else that evokes the tone of a midwestern mommy blog from 2004.

My G-Spot

It's in there, buddy.

Keep lookin'.

Mini-Meltdowns

On rare occasions, you might witness what looks like a totally irrational episode of tears and screaming. Don't worry. It's healthier than it looks. Catharsis may not be pretty, but it's absolutely necessary.

I'm Hopelessly in Love with Los Angeles.

It still makes me weak in the knees.

My Two Cell Phones

My business cell phone is named Fuck Stick. My personal cell phone is named Cunt Hair. Thought you should know.

{ I'm Not Materialistic. }

I like pretty things.

There's a difference.

On Days When I'm Not Living My Dream,

I take comfort in the knowledge that at least I'm living someone else's.

Delicate Sensibilities

Sometimes I think everyone in my world should just get a fucking helmet.

I Vote.

And one day, I want to vote for a brilliant and badass woman who's made a sex tape, done lots of drugs, and doesn't believe in God.

I Don't Exist to Make You a Better Man,

and your self-improvement isn't what makes me a good woman. That just happens to be a side effect of my integrity, grace, and high standards. You're welcome.

NOTES ON THE GOOD STUFF

Hey, dude.

I've always been a hot mess leading a charmed life in my own little corner of paradise, and it's important to me that you can keep up. It's also important that you come to know all of me, and that I can show you my whole and true self. I want you to know me completely, from the ridiculous to the profane, and all wild and crazy parts in between.

I'm a big fan of the pursuit of happiness, and I couldn't be happier that you're pursuing it with me. I'm not the sentimental type, so I probably won't ever tell you this enough, but thanks. It takes a really special man to put up with my shit, and I fucking love you.

Here are a few notes on the good stuff:

Intelligence

Every day I'm thankful that you're not one of those people who says "for all intensive purposes" or misuses the word "literally."

Backs

I got yours for life, 'cause I'm a ride-or-die bitch.

Aging

I promise to do it gracefully if

you promise not to freak out

when I get gray pubes.

Our Careers

I know I'm the free-spirited one,
but you're not allowed to be doing
something with your life that makes
you miserable. Sorry. We'll fucking live
in a box. It's fine.

Chuck Norris

He ain't got nothin' on you.

As You Wish

Every once in a while, I'm gonna turn to you out of the blue and say, "Farm boy, fetch me that pitcher." You'd better know the proper response.

Existential Potholes

Don't worry. I've got a spare tire in case your ego hits one too hard.

Three-Day Weekends

Sailor Jerry, barbecue, hotel pools, the beach, and at least one titty bar. You're my partner in crime, giddy up!

Kegel Exercises

You'll thank me later.

Inside Jokes

Remember that thing from that guy in that place that time? That shit was hilarious.

Marry/Fuck/Kill

I already married you, but there will still be days when I won't know whether to fuck you or kill you.

Nerding Out

Instead of that *Star Wars* marathon, how about I pretend your cock is a light saber and go down on you while humming the theme song? Okay fine, we can do both.

LCD Sound System

We may never have gotten to go to a concert together, but maybe one day there will be a James Murphy/David Byrne live collaboration that will blow our minds.

Nap Time

Close the curtains. Get in bed. Come on, let's do this.

Quid Pro Quo

I'll help scratch your seven-year
itch if you help scratch mine.

Regrets

are for couples who tell each other no.

Alibis

Not to sound all *Mob Wives*, but you
can always count on me for one.

Secrets

I'm the one you always tell.

Whee!

Make me say it as often as possible.

Yoga

Make fun of it all you want, but
that shit is why I can bend both
legs behind my head.

The Hangover Trifecta

Snacks, naps, and oral sex. You cure mine, and I'll cure yours.

Youth

Let's squeeze every last drop of excitement out of our youth, but let's not chase after it.

Up Shit's Creek

I got a paddle right here for you, boo.

Rainy Days

Fuck that noise, it's time for a bed party.

{ I Looked Hot Today. }

So did you.

ONE FINAL NOTE ON HAPPILY EVER AFTER

*H*ey, dude.

As my future husband, no doubt you'll appreciate how ridiculous all of this has been, especially any talk of our happily ever after. We both know there's no such thing. Not really. "I do" is not a pair of magic words, life is not a Disney cartoon, and a storybook marriage is overrated. That kind of thing is as boring and safe and artificial as a teacup ride.

This isn't me being pessimistic, quite the opposite. I'm all about the pursuit of happiness, and I'm totally open to having a life partner to chase it with me. If you really do exist, I won't be surprised if we end up raising all kinds of hell while growing old together. We just won't treat our marriage like it's a preamble to some eventual and nebulous state of bliss, because happiness is not some far-off thing in the distance.

Our happily ever after is right now, this very moment. Wherever you are. Wherever I am. This is it. It starts the second we realize it, and that goes for everybody.

If you're out there, I hope you're having as much fun with your life as I am, because I'm over here having an absolute blast, and if you happen to be standing in front of me at the bookstore with a cute smirk on your face after skipping to the last page like I knew you would, this is the moment where you're supposed to kiss me full on the lips.

Now go buy this book and take me to dinner. We've got a lot to talk about.

ACKNOWLEDGMENTS

This silly little book has its roots in an even sillier little Tumblr-based blog called "To My Husband" that I started a year ago with the help of a group of the most brilliant and hilarious single-lady bloggers I've ever had the pleasure of knowing.

My most heartfelt thanks and respect go out to Christine Friar, Erin Ryan, Heather Watson, Mari DeMonte, Marissa Ross, Nicole James, Caragh Poe, Tess Lynch, and Molly McAleer for their contributions to "To My Husband." You are all incredibly talented writers, and your future husbands are the luckiest dudes on the planet. Additional warm and fuzzies go out to John Jannuzzi for giving me so much earnest inspiration with his blog, "To My Wife."

I also want to thank Brandi Bowles at Foundry Media and Shana Drehs at Sourcebooks for making this book happen. It was a real pleasure working with such sharp and creative professionals, and although we haven't met, just know I always pictured you as Molly Shannon and Amy Sedaris from season five of *Sex and the City*. Of course, this book would never have gotten finished without my Venice Beach BFF. The stripper pole in your breakfast nook has magical powers.

Last but not least, I want to thank Milana Rabkin, Joel Begleiter, and the rest of the kick-ass team at United Talent Agency, as well as Dave "The Godfather" Feldman at Bloom Hergott. You guys rock so hard, I can't even tell you.

Stay wild, bitches.